OLAV H. HAUGE
LEAF-HUTS AND SNOW-HOUSES

Olav H. Hauge
Leaf-Huts and Snow-Houses

SELECTED POEMS
TRANSLATED BY

Robin Fulton

Anvil Press Poetry

Published in 2003
by Anvil Press Poetry Ltd
Neptune House 70 Royal Hill London SE10 8RF
www.anvilpresspoetry.com
Reprinted in 2010

ISBN 978 0 85646 357 0

This book is published
with financial assistance from
Arts Council England

The publisher gratefully acknowledges a subvention
from NORLA (Norwegian Literature Abroad)

A catalogue record for this book
is available from the British Library

Designed and set in Monotype Joanna by Anvil

CONTENTS

from *Ask the Wind* (1971)

from *A Few Blades of Grass* (1980)

INTRODUCTION

OLAV H. HAUGE (1908–1994), gardener by profession, spent almost his entire life in his native community of Ulvik, in the Hardanger region of Western Norway. His seven collections of poems, published between 1946 and 1980 and amounting to over four hundred pieces, are now regarded as among the most admired achievements of twentieth-century Norwegian letters. While working round the year he made time for reading and learning – he taught himself English, French and German to the extent that he produced fine translations from a wide range of poets in all three languages. His *Collected Poems* was supplemented by a gathering of his translations, the final version, in 1992, containing over two hundred poems. The most strongly represented names are Hölderlin, Trakl, Brecht, Celan, Stephen Crane, Robert Bly and twenty-one other poets are included with shorter selections, such as Johannes Bobrowski, Carl Sandburg, Robinson Jeffers, Kenneth Rexroth, Sylvia Plath, Yeats, T.E. Hulme, Rimbaud, Michaux and Char.

His published poems and translations occupy under five hundred pages, and the individual items are nearly all short and compact. By contrast, his "private" writings, his correspondence and his diary, were voluminous. Living where he did, the post was vital to him. Published letters include those to Bodil Cappelen (who became his wife) and to the poet and critic Jan Erik Vold, who did much to promote interest in Hauge's work. The diaries were published in 2000, in five enormous volumes, running to well over three thousand pages. He kept this chronicle from the age of fifteen right up to a week or so before his death, filling a total of eighty-four jotters. The result is voluminous only in terms of size: there are no rambling philosophizings. The entries tend to be curt, usually factual: details of correspondence, visitors, books read, quotations from books,

NOTE: Hauge's name is pronounced as two syllables, "How-ge", the g hard as in "good".

and the occasional dry but eloquent comment of the kind that puts complicated matters into a clear perspective.

Hauge wrote in a variety of nynorsk heavily influenced by the usage of his native locality. Historically nynorsk owed much to Ivar Aasen (1813–1896), whose aim was to salvage and regenerate what was more indigenous Norwegian as a counterbalance to the more dominant Danish-based bokmål. The language forms have equal status, legally, but books written in bokmål will often have the advantage of a bigger readership. If Hauge had written in bokmål like Rolf Jacobsen it is certain that the attention he was given later in his life would have come to him much sooner. Probably the language divide in Norway need not concern the reader of an English translation. It may well concern Norwegians who see their authors from either form being translated into the same kind of standard English. To Norwegians there is a world of difference between the bokmål of Rolf Jacobsen and the nynorsk of Hauge. The translator is concerned too, for there seems to be no viable manner of mirroring this difference in English. Resorting to dialect for one form would simply be misleading.

Visitors to Ulvik and its surroundings are duly impressed by the vast slabs of rock-face, the deep fjords, the apple-blossom in spring and the laden branches in autumn. This is the environment in which Hauge worked, and which he could describe with great accuracy. But the Ulvik and its surroundings which he recreated in his poems is something else, a parallel or superimposed or infiltrated reality of his own. At their best, his poems make this private Ulvik feel as tangible as the public one.

He certainly felt a very close connection between the making of poems and the carrying out of everyday, close-at-hand tasks. We could look at three poems from his 1966 collection that touch on this. In one of them he describes Brecht's verse as "handy to step into," like the pair of wooden clogs Hauge and his neighbours would keep out on the doorstep, ready for use. "Verse" reads:

> If you can turn a verse
> a farmer can approve of

you should be content.
A smith you can never fathom.
The worst to please is a joiner.

And "I Have Three Poems" ends:

A good poem
should smell of tea.
Or of raw earth and newly split firewood.

Then we can look at "I See You've Learnt" (1971):

I like
you
to use
few words,
few words and
short sentences
that drift
like a rain shower
down the page
with light and air
between.
I see you've learnt
to stack
a wood-pile in the forest,
good to build it
tall
then it'll dry;
if you build it long and low
the wood will rot.

We might have expected him to see the stacking up of the logs
as a paradigm of the well-made poem, and perhaps that meaning
is included here too – though the primary parallel with poetry
is the shower of rain. I doubt if Hauge is generally regarded as
enigmatic, but there are some of his poems (this being one of
them) which I have looked at on and off for about thirty years
now and each time I look I feel something very unsimple may
be going on behind the apparent simplicity.

There are a few poems, especially in the second half or so of his output, that seem to be simply happy, or happily simple, like "Winter Morning" (1966):

> When I woke today the panes were iced
> but I was warmed by a good dream.
> And the stove spread warmth in the room
> from a log it had kept cosy with all night.

or "Spring in the Mountains" (1966), "Time to Gather In" (1971), "The Old Poet Has Made a Verse" (1971, and "Sleep" (1980).

Such poems are not as easy to write as their manner might suggest, and they have a more subtle dimension when seen within the context of Hauge's work as a whole. This is partly because "pure" joy is often presented as being closely bound with sadness or worry (see "A Letter's Coming" (1971) or "I'll Have to Think of Doing Something Wrong" (1980)). It is also because, especially in his earlier work, there are strong undercurrents of coldness and despair. We are sometimes made aware of these rather abruptly. To take two small instances from his 1961 collection, "Smoke" ends

> But I sat often
> dark
> as Cain.

and "It's Cold in Big Houses" contains the line

> Then it looms bleakly, my loneliness,

then in "Spring by the Fjord" (1966) we read:

> my sorrows are at pasture
> black snow
> stifling the heather.

The poems don't try to tell us why such bleak feelings rise to the surface. I doubt if Hauge would ever have wanted to be "confessional", so we are probably meant to take his word for it that he has bouts of anguish, and not pry into eventual specific causes. I think too that Hauge belonged to a generation and a society to whom "private" means just that. Even so, a certain puzzlement awaits the reader now and then – how much, for instance, did he intend us to read into the terse little poem "I Have Lived Here" (1971):

> I have lived here more than a generation.
> Years with wind and stars in the high rigging
> have sailed past.
> Trees and birds have settled down here,
> but I have not.

The last line is so blunt it can feel defiant in the way it offers no explanation at all. To begin with we assume "here" means Ulvik; the years have sailed past leaving the poet where he started. There is nothing in the poem to encourage us to look for a wider context, where "here" could mean something like "this earth", but there is nothing to discourage us either – except a feeling that Hauge shied away from large gestures, especially as the years passed.

We could be tempted to toy with similar questions in "Leaf-Huts and Snow-Houses" (1971). The first four lines seem to go against his feeling for the craftsmanlike care demanded by the making of verses:

> There's not much to
> these verses, only
> a few words piled up
> at random.

If this is merely a gesture of modesty then, as we know, the modesty he felt about his work was genuine. Several diary entries in the winter of 1985–86 make clear his astonishment, even incredulity, that Anvil Press Poetry should publish a volume of his poems in English, he himself being a totally unknown foreigner. On 22 March 1986 he confided to his diary that he regarded his poems as no more than stubs and fragments and in the same entry he recorded his inability to understand why on earth I had sacrificed so much time translating his poems . . . The poem continues:

I think
nonetheless
it's fine
to make them, then
for a little while
I have something like a house.
I remember leaf-huts
we built
when we were small:
to creep in and sit
listening to the rain,
feel alone in the wilderness,
drops on your nose
and your hair –
Or snow-houses at Christmas,
to creep in and
close the hole with a sack,
light a candle and stay there
on cold evenings.

I'm not sure if Hauge would have wanted us to gloss the
poem by remarking on poetry as something which can give us
temporary refuge in an alien world. And anyway we might note
that the children are not unhappy. Nevertheless, the children are
being recollected a long time afterwards, perhaps with nostal-
gia, and the poem as a whole comes close to tempting us to see
both the verses and the human beings as *sub specie aeternitatis*.

A WORD OR TWO of explanation about this book is necessary.
In 1985 Anvil Press Poetry published a selection containing 119
poems translated by me plus 23 translations by James Greene.
In 1990 White Pine Press (New York State) published another
selection, this one containing 78 poems in my translation. Both
of these are out of print and what I have done now is to collate
my translations from the two books, revise many and add a few.
Counting titles, just under half of Hauge's total is available here
(194 out of 428).

Making a selection of a poet's work to be read in translation by foreigners differs in many fundamentals from making a selection for native readers. In the former case part of the selection process is dictated by questions of what can be reasonably translated in a narrow sense and what can be exported in the wider sense. Any one of an enormous range of obstacles may appear in the most unexpected and apparently unproblematic circumstances.

My selection contains only a couple of dozen pieces from Hauge's first three collections: the bulk of my choices are from his later four, those which appeared in 1961 (22 out of 50), 1966 (66 out of 107), 1971 (52 out of 82) and 1980 (27 out of 38). One reason for this is that a fair deal of his earlier work is metrical and rhyming. I have been trying to translate poems for close on forty years and have never seen a satisfactory way round the problem of what do with rhyme in translation. I find most of the arguments in favour of translating rhymed verse as rhymed verse in general convincing: a non-rhyming Dante, we think, can't possibly mirror Dante's use of his language. Yet apart from a very few instances I remain unconvinced by the practical results of putting those arguments into effect. Too often, too much is sacrificed for the sake of the rhyme.

The more highly-wrought nature of Hauge's earlier poems reflects the poetic traditions in which he began to write. In an interview (*Stavanger Aftenblad*, 5 May 1988) Hauge recalls that in his formative years his poetic horizon was dominated by the generation of writers who were born in the 1880s and whose books appeared before World War One. He mentions four names from the bokmål side of the language divide – Olaf Bull (1883–1933), Herman Wildenvey (1886–1959), Alf Larsen (1885–1967) and Arnulf Øverland (1889–1968), and then four from the nynorsk side – Olav Aukrust (1883–1929), Olav Nygard (1884–1924), Tore Ørjasæter (1886–1968) and Kristofer Uppdal (1878–1961). Only the last named was in touch with international modernism and his poetry was perhaps less widely read than that of the others listed. Modernism arrived late in Norway: it reached Finland before Sweden, and Sweden before

Norway. "Not that I didn't read the modernists," he says. "In English anthologies I read both Eliot and Pound long before the war, but I wasn't so interested. I preferred traditional poets like Yeats and Hardy." He goes on to mention his fondness for translations of Chinese poetry, a fondness that left many traces in his own poems.

A second and better reason for concentrating on Hauge's work from the 1960s onwards is that it is in the formally less elaborate poems that his individual poetic personality finds greater expression. Although his mentors were important to him there is a broad trend in his work over the decades away from word-play and towards a more colloquial though still measured mode of address. Perhaps Hauge thought the same – for example, in 1988 his publishers brought out a double cassette of him reading 99 poems of his own choice: only 19 of the 99 employ rhyme, and of those that do, eight are sonnets.

I suspect Hauge might have agreed with the following comment I recently came across, from the Uruguayan poet Circe Maia: "it seems to me that if poetry is considered too much as a linguistic experiment, that other element, experience of life, the essential, may be absent."

ROBIN FULTON

Postscript, 2010

MANY POETS are forgotten in the years after their death but in Hauge's case the opposite has happened. He has so far been represented, often substantially, in Chinese, Danish, Dutch, English, Faroese, French, German, Hebrew, Hindi, Hungarian, Icelandic, Italian, Korean, Russian, Serbian and Spanish. Many of his poems have been set to music by Norwegian musicians, and Vigdis Nielsen's film/DVD on Hauge and his background, *The Other Man* (Flimmer Films, 2008) has been widely shown.

from *Embers in the Ashes* (1946)

BLACK CROSSES

Black crosses
in white snow
stooped in rain, awry.

Here came the dead
over the thorny moor
with crosses on their shoulders
and laid them by
and went to rest
under each icy tussock.

THE BIRCH

Birch
in pinewood
– a green banner
when spring is young.
But the pine is
dark and sad.

The birch
persists
– is at last
a bright blaze.
But the pine is no
less heavy.

Then the birch drops
the yellow leaves
and is left there
cold
with rime
on naked twigs.

THE RIVER-GIRL

On bright spring nights
when the sap is rising
in the birches
she tosses her hair
and sings
and dances before the mountain.
Now her game is over,
with white arms she hugs
the iron grey cliff
in a long
sucking ice-kiss.

I SHAKE SNOW OFF YOUNG TREES

What is one to do when
it comes down on one,
heave clumsy spears
at the dancing
tumbling flocks,
or hunch shoulders
and take what comes?

In the twilight I bounce
through the garden
with a pole,

to help.
It takes
so little:
a sharp tap
with the pole
or a jerk
in a twig-end –
you have the loose snow
all over you while
the apple-tree has sprung
back up
straight again.

They're so proud, young trees,
they haven't learned
to stoop
to anything but wind –
and it's all
just fun
and a thrill.
Trees that have borne crops
can take an armful of snow
and think nothing of it.

THIN ICE

The fjord had stilled
after the autumn storm.
Now it lay mirroring
spaces and stars,
and the moon spread it
with gold.

And one night
the black shining depth
took a covering of steel
– for shelter.
Bore birds
and thrown stones
and let snow lie.
What was land,
what was water?

Till winter storm
and deep currents
suddenly splintered
the steel surface
and pounded it to mush.

. . .

Mind, where is your peace,
your purposes, your ties?
Thin ice
on a sleeping sea.

BENEATH THE CRAG

You live beneath a crag,
knowing you do.
But you sow your acre
and make your roofs fast
and let your children play
and you lie down at night
as if it weren't there.

One summer evening
perhaps
as you lean on your scythe
your eye will skim
across the crag
where they say
the crack is,
and perhaps one night
you'll lie awake
listening for
a falling stone.

And when the rock-slip comes
it will not be a surprise.
But you'll set to and clear
the green patch
beneath the crag
– as life allows.

THE FIRE MOUNTAIN

Don't be too mocking,
harmless decent hills!
Through miserable me
could burst all the shut-
in power
of our original
craggy lineage.

It was not my lava,
my ash, my fire
more than yours,
but the flaw was mine.

I am only a mountain
like others,
no riddle
no godhead,
only a run-down
burnt-out heap.
But no one
knows as I
what forces
in us sleep.

BEHIND THE MOUNTAIN OF LONELINESS

Loneliness is sweet –
so long as the road back
to the others
is open.
You don't shine
for yourself alone.

But that day the mountain
falls shut
behind you,
you'll stand calling
in blind anguish
and beating your knuckles
on a closed wall.

And you'll appeal to the stars,
the stones, the sea and the wind,
thinking they know
and making yourself
of less account than they are.

You – behind the mountain of loneliness!
A hidden stream
runs back
if only like Sinbad
you dared to follow it.

THE STONE GOD

You carry the stone god
within you.
You give him loyal service
and secret offerings.
Wreaths and lit candles
you bring him
with bloody hands,
yet still feel
the coldness of him
in your heart,
know your breath
hardens like his
and your smile
as chilled.

YOU WANT ONLY TO BE

No root groping
in the hard rock,
no sprout, no sapling,
not the strong bole in the storm,
no humble branch,
no bast, no bark
in frost and snow –
no rising sap,

no force to grow,
no fruit, no seed,
not the leaf quietly
building its dome –
you want only to be
the swaggering bloom.

THE SEA

That was the sea.
Solemnity itself,
vast and grey.
But as the mind
in solitary moments
suddenly opens up
shifting mirror-views
of mysterious depths –
the sea too
one blue morning
can open itself
to sky and solitude.
Look, the sea glitters,
and I too have stars
and blue depths.

THE FISHERMAN AND THE SEA

Mysterious
is the sea in man's mind.
To be a humble fisherman there
was my prayer
and my dream.

With search-lights
and plummets
you came wanting
to drag my sea.

To drag where
there's no bottom.
Rock then, sea of my sorrow!
And may depths
and distant stars
baffle his toil.

TONGUE AND BELL

I'm the tongue
in the bell,
the heavy
silent
tongue.

Don't touch me —
don't let
my nudging
against the iron
splinter
the silence.

Only when the bell
starts swinging
will I beat,
swing
and beat
on
the deep
iron.

from *Slowly the Woods Redden in the Gorge*
(1956)

STEEL

Will is steel.
Unsheathed and blue.
The steel stays then
in a willed thought,
a willed feeling,
a willed deed.

Most beautiful the thought
without steel,
most tender the feeling
which lacks it,
most handsome the deed
which does without it.

Will is our hidden steel,
the sharp edge against fate,
a lever which can prise
mountains aside.
But we don't like
baring it.

It's play we love
and children and flowers in the wind –
and we regard with awe
the heavy pull of tides,
and mountains that fall . . .

ONE THING YOU KNEW

One thing you knew:
that the world's folly is a mountain
which could well endure your onslaughts
and that no-one gave
more heed to
your words, than
to the dog
across the fjord.

You wouldn't give guidance
to anyone – only incite
against the crag,
that porous mountain
which just grows and grows
until it's all
that's left.

When you noticed they began
listening to you,
you were dumb;
it can't have been the gneiss
you'd set upon.

And you who knew
that the world's folly
is an icy sneering sword-proof mountain
and that the way to wisdom
is endless!

DO ANOTHER MAN A FAVOUR

He came down from the hills, wanted home,
got himself ferried from Osa
out to Øydvinstò.
And he was open-handed
and offered to pay.

But the man from Osa
was not for sale.
I want to pay;
I can't reach you
to do you a favour.
Then do another man
a favour,
said the man from Osa
and shoved off.

SHOW US YOUR FIELD OF RYE

Don't meet us with:
barking watchdog,
threatening fist,
keep-off-the-crop!
But one morning early
show us your field of rye!

KIN

If you're kin with the birch
you'll manage long enough,
you'll thole both wind and rain
and the ground biting your hair.
But you won't always be
as bright and straight;
the birch on the scree
is lumpy and twisted
and black in the twigs.

If you're kin with the pine
you'll manage too,
and the poorer the soil
the longer you'll last;
but your heartwood is brittle
and you are heavy in storms
and morose under snow.

If you're kin with matgrass
you'll manage longest:
yellow and green in the beard,
quick-tempered and tough as hell;
nothing bothers you
– and no-one wants you!

SEVEN WINDS

Seven winds, seven winds
hummed and sang.
Seven winds, seven winds
found the heavens too small.

Seven winds, seven winds
clashed in squalls.
A wild reel there was,
and dead leaves swirled.

Seven winds, seven winds
went their ways.
And all the winds
are asleep today.

PUTTING OUT

The sea heaves in the dark.
Put out now?
Can't.
Yes, right now.
The night opens, makes space.
A wall's building up in the west.
The moon comes out and shines –
right now.

It falls and falls
today as yesterday,
falls in cliffs
where only the eagle
swoops –
falls without pause,
falls heavily against
rock,
with no sound,
with no song,
struggles and falls –
spills out of
gorges and clefts,
bubbles
in the white beard,
stops
and hangs –
falls
in timelessness,
falls
trapped in its bad dream –
can't get a word out,
not one sound . . .

MEETING

They met – not certain if
they should greet each other.
But she spoke then, walked
a step or two along with him,
one doesn't recognize
everyone after dark.
She was still young,
the gleam in her eyes
just as black.

Words fell
like sinkers
from the gunwale of each boat
with open sea between.

Only afterwards he noticed
that they'd tangled
somewhere in the depths
where the currents tugged
over treacherous forests of seaweed
and abrupt chasms.

How wary she was!
And quick to break off.

But then he had the broken line-end
and her hook,
even if he didn't know
a life-line
thrown to him.

SLOWLY THE TRUTH DAWNS

To waken, and feel
your heart sink
heavy and dark
and hardening . . .

Slowly the sea lifts its billow,
slowly the forest reddens in the gorge,
slowly the flames begin to lick in hell,
slowly the truth dawns.

A SEAGULL

A seagull
you were, and that you
should end like this!
The others rise in the storm,
you stand on a skerry screeching.

THERE'S STILL TIME

It's old shadows
you sing for,
shadows of
yourself.

Unborn visions threaten
your day – when
will you give them
life?

There's still time,
you think
– the grass is still
green.

SPRING FJORD

There's something grim in his gift,
something vile and strange
in the bottle-green growth
the spring sun doesn't want to know about:
fronds, grown in another world,
with rotten-smelling ooze, and rank
sediment and slimy stone and
weed-tangle crawling up
from black depths.
And it's true, the green velvet border

he tries to give to the pale shores
was woven under ice; they've long since had
grass and buttercups,
he thought.

But in the twilight his generosity shines,
a green edge of soft velvet
round frozen lands. And the weaver
has withdrawn warily
and shut his eye.

RADIANT SPACES

Holy star!
Spaces of cold radiance
you spread round you,
cold radiance.

The great experience too
spreads spaces
of radiance
round itself,
safeguarding
the kernel of light.

Don't come close,
never come close!
For all time
spaces of radiance
shall remain between.

from On the Eagle's Tussock (1961)

SINGING AGAIN

The river deep in my mind is singing again,
and windless calm reaches me from cool night-country
where dream-blue pinnacles mirror themselves
in other seas.

But what are my words?
Storm-twisted forests
facing north,
craggy rocks
facing day's
harrowing
fire.

DON'T GIVE ME THE WHOLE TRUTH

Don't give me the whole truth,
don't give me the sea for my thirst,
don't give me the sky when I ask for light,
but give me a glint, a dewy wisp, a mote
as the birds bear water-drops from their bathing
and the wind a grain of salt.

I OPEN THE CURTAIN

Before going to bed I open the curtain,
I want to see the living darkness when I wake,
and the forest and the sky. I know a grave
without a peep-hole to the stars.

Orion's come in the west, forever on the hunt –
he's come no further than I.
The cherry tree outside is bare and black.
In the huge blue curve of heaven
the morning moon draws with a hard nail.

TO A MOUNTAIN

It's as if I've never seen you before, yet I've had
your stubborn claw in view all my days,
mountains are mountains, and the Lord has weighed
    them.
Grandeur I have seen and calm,
my own arrogance facing the infinite;
a sign explained.

But early this morning I saw you: you were like an eagle
waiting for sunrise, ready to fly.
Now you have folded your broad wings
behind the forest tops. And the dusk
and the stars are yours.

ON THE SHORE

She gave no answer, but turned her back to you – and
    went.
And the wind and the clouds, yes even the sea turned
    its back
darkening; the stones on the shore dived,
each straw, each wave made off
for another shore.

EVENING CLOUDS

Here come the clouds
with greetings from
distant shores,
it's long since
they had any news for me.
Blushing
high in the evening sky,
no doubt all for
someone else.
So – there are still
hopes left
in the world.

THE MESSAGE STICK

Would come, you knew.
Had to come.
And now was here.

You trembled,
joy sang in you.
But your loneliness raised
walls
higher than heaven.

You think so often of
that message-stick.
Such
golden wings.

THE SAWHORSE

Strong-bodied, straddling,
he lifts fresh-hewn horns
and waits for logs and saw,
logs and saw.
He – who himself has been
a swaying storm,
a living
bright dream.

Sawdust piles up around him
in rotting heaps,
saw-teeth rasp
his back and he becomes
gashed and skew-legged and grey.
Winter and summer he stands in the yard,
with the chopping-block for company.

God knows what the night
tells him,
God knows
what he broods over
out under the stars.

THE STORY OF CH'Ü YÜAN

This is the story of Ch'ü Yüan. The king's adviser.
Rice-fields and mandarins bowed before him.
Until he was sacked and became a dreamer.

Where was his kingdom now? On stars and fabled
isles,
far from here, in search of her he saw in a dream.
Preferred to visit the other world. And as adviser
set crosses and signs for strange roads and drew
on silk markers and omens for those who come after.

But Ch'ü Yüan complained. He could not forget
his country and the people he served; nowhere
did the orange tree blossom as by his native wells.

I don't know why he complained. But I do know
that reality's a hard shore for a ship-wrecked dreamer.
And the dew makes the water widest.
Did he miss the bridge hanging so high in the air?

What was he thinking when he clasped a stone and leapt
in the Li-mo river?

The river runs, gave no answer,
the staring stone eye sank into contemplation.

TO LI PO

To rule in The Heavenly Empire
no doubt enticed you, Li Po.
Didn't you have the whole world, the clouds and
     the wind,
and blessedness in your intoxication?
Even greater, Li Po, is it
to rule over one's own heart.

ROCK-SLIP

If you're smiling
it's far away
— in a glint of sun
on cold snow.

Only high and serious,
that's you. Who'd think
you'd freeze loose your breast-knot
in heavy murderous rock?

Dangerous and loose,
these stones.
You stand listening to them
as they come —
hear them thunder in the woods
beneath you, ripping up
peeled trunks and rasping heather-clumps
and suchlike innocent creeping things
— hurling them with you
into the gorge.

While you — you hold your head
up in the blue, cool your brow
in stiff cold winds
and whistle.

SMOKE

The smoke rises cheerfully
from a chimney in the woods
where the young couple live.

With glad hearts they offer
stout fir
hard birch
to the powers of light.

In the miser's farm the smoke
is meagre and thin:
lean years,
little left
for God.

You don't see
your own smoke.
But I sat often
dark
as Cain.

AN OLD-FASHIONED NORWEGIAN

I always greet matgrass like an old acquaintance,
not that he was all that friendly, I recall
how he pricked through my woollen shirt when we
    carried dry hay,
but a good taskmaster he made
for a novice fumbling with a sickle;
outlying fields are now his habitat.

Nardus stricta he's called in Latin.
I knew him long before I learned that
fancy name, he was a cross-patch
the scythe wouldn't take,
tops white,
roots yellow with ants,
wiry and flint-blue –
the only way to take him was
before the sun was high, when
he'd be lop-
eared in the dew.

I read about an old-fashioned Norwegian.
Matgrass is that sort,
thrives in drought and sun
on scrawny soil
– feed him fertilizer
and he'll fade away.

THE CHOPPING-BLOCK

Hard to be
block under axe,
I've felt.
But I learned
when they chose
just me:
Stand still and keep quiet!

Up the slope my brother stumps
are putting out new leaves.
Let them chop away
here in the yard!
I swagger and strut
in my splintery crown.

IT'S COLD IN BIG HOUSES

It's cold in big houses.
I notice that in autumn
when the first snowflakes start falling
and the ground hardens under frost.
Then it looms bleakly, my loneliness,
and the roof is full of cracks,
and the axe-blow yelps in the frozen forest.

My forest is a forest
in its forest,
my mountain a mountain
in its mountain,
and the day is a glint
in its night.
The few people and animals I meet,
pottering in the gloom with pine needles and sprigs
and leaving their footprints in the rime,
are shadowy glimmers in its dream.

WINTER DAY

What does this alien light want here?
The day is under white stars.
And the dreams sprout under the moon.

The mountain has words far inside itself,
but its breast is stiff and beard frozen.
The river-mouth answers with brief glints, open a
    brief moment,
and the firs give up a little resin.
The goldcrest shakes down snow,
and the horse's frosty muzzle quivers.
The firewood twists out cold stiff fat,
and the frost eats up the axe-blow.

But now the peak butts the sun's disc into a thousand
    splinters, knocks
its squinting glance towards a distant sphere.

High spruce-candles on the ridges snuff out
and trees settle down in groves for the night.
The river sighs in the gorge, chills into ice its yearning
    for the sea,
and the stones sleep beneath the snow with green
    dreams in their hearts.

SNOW EVENING

Give away your darkness and be rich.
Like an evening after snow.
The ground is rich and the slopes,
the pine-needles laden,
and the houses are rich, secure
for life and warmth.

The sleeping earth knows
of its splendour.
The heavens' frosted eyebrows
are full of stars.

BENEATH THE STARS

What is it that has driven me out
beneath this hard morning sky?
These blue demanding stars,
what is it they want?

The hills promise nothing – just
give way, letting the fjord fill up
and the rivers run down. The hills
feel nothing beneath the snow.

But the wooded slopes are prostrate
baring their need beneath the stars.
It's my own pain, my own hurt
lying there black as iron and bleeding
and vowing to turn green again and sing.

WINTER STILL LIVES IN THE LIGHT

Winter still lives in the light
and beds down in the first grass,
it is ice-green and cold
after him when he rises.
And when the cherry trees come
they come with snow and lay
sisterly cheeks against the glaciers.
The dandelion saws through last year's straw
and kindles frost-yellow bonfires.

SPRUCE FOREST

Hungering he climbs from dark valleys to the heights,
he has behind him all the sorrows of earth: –
Kindle our tops, quicken our lights!
And heaven opens an eye
turns to another firmament.
The perplexed forest fumbles in its own darkness,
a few frozen stars hanging in the meagre tops.

SONG, TREAD LIGHTLY ON MY HEART

Song, tread lightly on my heart,
tread lightly as bell-heather on watery moor,
as bird on overnight ice.
Break the crust of pain,
song, and you'll drown.

THE CORNFIELD

An old woodcut of Tower Bridge
and an oleograph of a cornfield.
No other pictures in Ward D.

Tower Bridge sooty above the river.
But it's the cornfield I watch.
A golden sea of corn.

Not like other fields. Have all
the day-dreaming eyes transported it
into their heaven?

An autumn-blue, mild heaven,
no harvesters, no scythe.

from *Drops in the East Wind* (1966)

THE TRUTH

The truth is a shy bird
a Roc
flying outside time,
sometimes before,
sometimes after.
Some say there's
no such thing,
those who have seen her
say nothing.
I have never thought of truth
as a tame bird,
but if she were
you could well stroke her feathers
and not frighten her into a corner till
she turns owlish eyes and claws against you.
Others say truth
is a cold knife-edge,
she is both
yin and yang,
the snake in the grass,
and the little wren who rises from the eagle
when the eagle thinks he's highest.
And I have seen
truth dead:
eyes like a frozen hare's.

EVERYDAY

You've left the big storms
behind you now.
You didn't ask then
why you were born,
where you came from, where you were going to,
you were just there in the storm,
in the fire.
But it's possible to live
in the everyday as well,
in the grey quiet day,
set potatoes, rake leaves,
carry brushwood.
There's so much to think about here in the world,
one life is not enough for it all.
After work you can fry bacon
and read Chinese poems.
Old Laertes cut briars,
dug round his fig trees,
and let the heroes fight on at Troy.

WE ARE NOT SAILING ON THE SAME SEA

We are not sailing on the same sea
though it looks like it.
Heavy timber and iron on deck,
sand and cement in the hold,

I'm low in the water,
make slow headway,
pitch in squalls,
wail in mist.
You're sailing in a paper boat,
your dream fills the blue sail,
so mild the wind, so meek the water.

IT DOESN'T MATTER

It doesn't matter
if the grasshopper whets his scythe.
But when the wood-louse whispers
watch out.

THE MOUNTAIN-WIND

You were a cold hard mountain-wind.
Until a dark windbreak rose up there
and splintered your force. Death.
Now you creep – a humbled wind
along lukewarm slopes.

ERRATIC BOULDER

A most remarkable place
to settle on, a bare rocky
slope, poised over
the cliff-drop.
Don't you appreciate your success?

IN MY FATHER'S HOUSE

In my Father's house are many rooms.
And many are the doors leading in.
What stairway will you creep up,
what tears will you let fall,
what bell will you toll,
will you use a sledge-hammer or beat
your knuckles bloody?
Do they open only for
horn brawl and trumpet blast?

There comes a moment
when the doors swing on their hinges, you don't know
if such a moment will come again.
But Odin let go of the keel
and *Romeo und Juliet auf dem Dorfe*
sailed into heaven on a haystack.

ACROSS THE SWAMP

You can walk safely
across the swamp
on the stumps of all the trees that have fallen here.
Roots like these last long, they could
have lain here for centuries,
and still there are mouldering traces
under the moss,
they're still there and take your weight
and let you cross unscathed.
And when you push out on the mountain lake
you feel how the memory of a cold person
who drowned himself here
is present too and bears the frail skiff,
the madman who trusted his life
to water and eternity.

THE OWL

Trees shine in the garden
with ripe berries,
the thrush flurries in.
And there sits the owl,
glowering with his round head.
The thrush jerks round, wings
discreetly off.
Although the owl's dead
and sits in the sun,
it's black as night and scary
in the tree where the owl is.

OPHELIA

You're no enigma, Ophelia,
only the puzzle a life and a heart are.
How stubborn and tangled life can be.
Where would we go
if we didn't have sorrow and death?
Dance, Ophelia, sing!
Scatter roses around you,
run away into a darker room,
it's sweeter there, the day there
not so hard.
When the fiery point of anguish stings you
sing, Ophelia, dance!
The moat is scattered with roses.

UP ON THE HEIGHTS

After long journeying on impassable roads
you are up on the heights.
Adversity failed to daunt you, you trod it
under you, rose higher.

That's how you see it. After life has tossed you
aside and you happened to land on the top,
like a one-footed wooden horse on the rubbish-heap.
Life is merciful, it blinds and dazzles
and fate shoulders your burdens:
folly and pride become crags and swamps,
hate and spite become wounds from the arrows of
        the envious,
and the doubt that chafed you becomes
cold dried-up gorges.

You step into the hut.
On the hearthstone the cauldron lies toppled,
its black feet sprawling and hostile.

KERB STONES *

Now and then the road
crosses a plain.
No fatal matter
if you don't follow it
but people do.
Most often there's a rockface
on the one side,
a precipice on the other,
so you must keep to it.
The rockface blocks you in,
the kerb stones leer
like a row of teeth:
Stick to the road!
Jagged kerb stones
blasted from the crags
by staunch quarrymen,
turn sharp edges
against you:
We'll split your skull.
You shall not tumble off.

* The stones referred to are *stabbesteinar*, rough-cut vertical slabs
of stone set up along the exposed outer edges of old highways.

ONE WORD

One word
– one stone
in a cold river.
One more stone –
I must have more
if I'm to get across.

THE WEATHERCOCK

The smith beat him
with tail and comb,
up he went,
the world was new
and the winds many.
He was keen,
wheeled, cawed,
puffed his feathers
at each gust,
in storms stood erect
with his long neck –
Till he rusted
and stuck, standing
skewed to the north.
From where most often
the winds come.

A GRAIN

A grain of justice took
root in my heart, grew
and became a salt fire.
I sacrificed to him, fattened him up
with meaty slaughter.
And the flame became a lizard.

WALL

A good wall can come
from old stones
if you lay them well
and make them fit in.
But perhaps they're badly cut
and uneven, lime or old cement
still hanging on, you can see
they were in a wall before.
Best to blast out new stone,
cut it the way you want
so it'll bond well
and look good.
Then you'll have a solid wall.
And you can say it's yours.

WINTER HAS FORGOTTEN

Winter has forgotten white cows on the mountain
where they graze on green slopes.
But the spring sun and the grass are too strong.
Each day the cows are thinner.

WINTER MORNING

When I woke today the panes were iced
but I was warmed by a good dream.
And the stove spread warmth in the room
from a log it had kept cosy with all night.

THE RIVERS MEET

The rivers meet, each from its mountain.
Grasp each other by the hand.
Blend their song and their blood.

On they go, of one mind, stronger,
less likely to stumble on the stones:
No one will wade us dry-shod now!

AND I WAS SORROW

And I was sorrow and stayed in a cave.
And I was pride and built beyond the stars.
Now I build in the nearest tree
and in the morning when I waken
the pine threads its needle with gold.

SPRING BY THE FJORD

The blue haze coils
up from ploughed squares,
the shore is green
this year too.
On shady slopes
my sorrows are at pasture
black snow
stifling the heather.

THE WIND HAS SO MUCH TO TELL
THIS SPRING

The wind has so
    much
        to tell

this spring, I haven't heard
    him
        for years,

he huffs
    and puffs
        in bare trees:

wills them to quicken
    and break into green!
        Cuffs the roof-ridge:

wills, wills them
    to quicken!
        And so he's

back in the trees,
    shaking them
        by the scruff

with a rough blast
    and a sharp!
        Teases

round corners,
    noses
        in last year's leaves

and flicks
     a twirl
          of them up –

they're dry now,
     dry –

scampers across
     the field, whirls up
          dust,

comes back, puts on
     an old black hat
          and is gone –

Come back!
     Come back!

SPRING IN THE MOUNTAINS

Today the snowdrifts
are dancing like stags in the sun.
The river is hurrying homewards
taking winter with it.
The golden plover has arrived
and green slopes of grass.

WILLOW

Willow
stands yellow
as it did last year
but fewer see it.
Nor do you hear
flutes now.

THE CAT

The cat will be
sitting in the farmyard
when you come.
Speak a little with him. On the farm
he's the one who knows what's what.

MORNING BY THE FJORD

The ferry breaks open
black unmoving water,
tips plate-metal
against green land.

AUTUMN FISHING

The river is flecked with ice,
she is thin
and bites hard
and rages between the stones.
The ash-stumps are grey
along the bank,
each shoot and black
bud showing up,
alder-brakes are ragged
and sagged down with rime.
The trout is wriggling,
is cold and firm.

THE ISLET

Solitary, exiled
far from land,
the islet toils
on a rough tarn.
On still nights
when the water sleeps
it feels the rock beneath,
spreads out heavy and huge,
becomes one with the land.

THE LOG

Pell
mell
it went, said the log.
Now I want to rest,
he finished up in a backwater.

SEED

No place to grow, this.
Don't put down roots,
don't put out flowers!
If you want to save your life
stay hard and whole!

SKERRIES

There are many skerries in the ocean.
Nonetheless it was
one
that saved you.

YOU WERE THE WIND

I am a boat
without wind.
You were the wind.
Was that the course I was to take?
Who cares about the course
with such a wind!

THE WINDMILL

The wings are made for catching wind,
no great gust need blow
before they turn and the works whirl.
In a storm I'd lash them
or take them off.
A naked stump would then
have struggle enough.

THIS RED SCAR

This red scar in the mask?
Of course it's ugly.
But useful:
Ram's horn,
radar screen,
bulldozer,
stump-puller
car bumper
– according to
whom
you have to face.

IN THE HEN-YARD

In the hen-yard you should
keep clear of
the Cock and the Top Hen,
don't blink,
don't stir a toe!
A mere nod from you
is a snake-bite.

ONE OUGHT

One ought
to crawl out
and loosen up
and brighten up
and strut,
do as the juniper
mock hail and rain!

THE RIVER RISES

The fish doesn't moan
if the river rises.
But the poor old beaver
panics over his houses.

THE SCYTHE

I am so old
I keep to the scythe.
It sings quietly in the grass
and thoughts can flow.
It doesn't hurt either
says the grass
to fall to the scythe.

THE SAW

Trash,
says the saw.
Fine firewood.
She says what
she thinks, the saw.

BERTOLT BRECHT

A versatile fellow:
playwright, actor, poet.
His verse was handy to step into,
it stood on the door-step
like a pair of wooden clogs.

WATCHMAN*

Watchman
waits for
the nibble
from beneath.
Will he hold?
Doesn't matter much
if the fish are small.
Frozen, he stands on the ice,
has always had to stand alone.
I like watchman.
He shows us what's biting out there.
More than that he can't.

* A stick to which the line is fastened in ice-fishing.

ARROW AND BULLET

Arrow came before bullet.
That's why I like arrow.
Bullet goes many miles.
But its crack is terrible.
Then arrow smiles.

THE SWORD

The sword
cuts
when it's drawn,
if nothing else
– then air.

NOTHING'S WRONG

Vassfjøro has put on
sack-cloth and ashes
and hides under its hood.
The other mountains bathe
in late evening sun, it's then
nothing's wrong.
Storms over the North Sea,
says the radio-forecast.

DON'T USE SANDPAPER

Don't use sandpaper where a well-aimed knife has cut,
don't re-route the ski-track that took you safely over
        the crags,
don't take back words once said.
Words are dynamite and work in the depths and on
        the heights,
in that crack they blasted
ground-water can rise.

VERSE

If you can turn a verse
a farmer can approve of
you should be content.
A smith you can never fathom.
The worst to please is a joiner.

OLD POET HAS A GO AT BEING A MODERNIST

He too had a mind to try
these new stilts.
He's got himself up,
steps warily like a stork.
Remarkable, how far-sighted.
He can even count his neighbour's sheep.

THE NESTING CLIFF

Perhaps you like being a nesting cliff.
It's fine with a bird or two, of course.
But to be such a restless raucous heap?
It must be vanity and foolishness that made
all these birds crowd together
and mess all over you.

I HAVE THREE POEMS

I have three poems,
he said.
Think of counting poems.
Emily tossed them
in a box, I
can't imagine she counted them,
she just spread out a tea-packet
and wrote a new one.
That was right. A good poem
should smell of tea.
Or of raw earth and newly split firewood.

WHAT I REMEMBER BEST

What I remember best from childhood
is the wind.
There's no wind left.
No wind
and no birds,
what'll happen now?

ROTTED TREE-STUMP

Everything soft in him
fungus and worm have gorged.
The hard, the tough, the twisted
remain. Knot and gnarl
still hold him up.

SUMMER NEARING ITS END

Foxgloves are ringing
the last red bells,
the evening wind is stroking
forgotten grass.

WHEN AUTUMN COMES

When autumn comes
when the cold comes
and the evenings turn dark,
I sit by the fire
and hum my song –
keep anguish alive,
coax out sunny memories.

THE MIRROR

When I was young
I'd look at myself
in the smithy window.
The heart sees itself
in God's mirror.
Which is smoky too.

THEY WANT AWAY

They want away
from earth, all of them.
The insect bustles,
and the worm peels off soil.

GREEN APPLES

Summer was cold and rainy.
The apples are green and flecked.
Yet I gather and sort them
and stack boxes in the cellar.
Green apples are better than none.
Where we live is 61° north.

THE MOUNTAIN

The mountain shows me his scars,
scoured stripes and claw-marks from frost.
Yet there were many days he drank the sun
and was stroked by a gentle wind.

THE ASPEN

I know how flint
comes into being
said the aspen and trembled
by the gate,
she is tough
as soaked timber.
And if what they say
is true there's such a thing
as a blue diamond.

THE BIRCH

He had noticed
one thing
said Old-Hallvor,
that the birch grows
only in the morning.
That I don't believe.
I believe one grows while sleeping.

BRIAR

The roses have been sung about.
I want to sing of the thorns
– and the root, that clings
hard to the rock, hard
like a thin girl's hand.

THE RAINBOWS

Bridge over bridge –
three rainbows!
Where shall we go,
do you suppose?

The first no doubt
leads to paradise,
the second ends up
in snow and ice.

The third? It came
this way
down into the garden
with you and me!

WHEN I WAKEN

When I waken, a black
raven hacks at my heart.
Shall I never again waken
to seas and stars, woods and night,
morning with birdsong?

PINE-TORCH

Pine-torch knows
much
and burns long
and bright,
can kindle others
and sees much
but takes no heed of that,
the flame is free –
the smoke is harsh
and stings
in nose and eye,
comes after:
I don't care
about thanks.

FLOOR

It's good to have
a floor of one's own.
Did it tremble
or did it suffer
under you?
Dance
I don't,
but I do pace
to and fro

busy with
my this and that.
I'm angry
now and then,
angry,
with a heavy tread,
there must be something
young
in me still,
young,
a wild horse that
whinnies in the reins.
And now and then the floor
resounds,
and there's a jingling from
cupboard and stove.

BLUE MUSICIANS

They stand there
their arms full
of music, the kind
they've inherited,
and fill the space in front
of them with a blue wind
and stand then in-
side this wind
and blow –
they are just
this blue wind.

They are
blue wind
until – is there
anything
left of them?
There –
the brass horn
didn't cackle,
but it was
about to.
The eyes
stare after
that note,
stand like
white dots.

IT'S THE DREAM

It's the dream we carry in secret
that something miraculous will happen,
that it must happen –
that time will open
that the heart will open
that doors will open
that the rockface will open
that springs will gush –
that the dream will open,
that one morning we will glide into
some little harbour we didn't know was there.

from *Ask the Wind* (1971)

OVERNIGHT THE GRASS HAS TURNED GREEN

Overnight the grass has turned green.
A bird is trying to sing,
mist rises,
and the sun comes over the snow-crest.
From mornings long ago
happiness beats faintly on its copper shield.

T'AO CH'IEN

If one day T'ao Ch'ien
came to visit me, I
would show him my cherry and apple trees,
and I'd prefer him to come in spring
when they're in blossom. Then we'd sit in the shade
with a glass of cider, perhaps I'll show him
a poem – if I can find one he'd like.
The dragons that blaze across the sky trailing poison
    and smoke
soared more quietly in his time, and more birds sang.
There's nothing here he'd not understand.
More than ever he'd want to retire
to a little garden like this.
But I don't know if he'd do so with a good conscience.

TIME TO GATHER IN

These mild days of sun in September.
Time to gather in. There are still tufts
of cranberries in the wood, the rose-hips redden
along the stone dykes, nuts fall at a touch,
and clumps of blackberries gleam in thickets,
thrushes poke about for the last redcurrants
and the wasp sucks away at the sweet plums.
In the evenings I set my ladder aside and hang
up my basket in the shed. Meagre glaciers
already have a thin covering of new snow.
Lying in bed I hear the throb of the brisling fishers
on their way out. All night, I know, they'll glide
with staring searchlights up and down the fjord.

I CHOPPED DOWN THE BIG APPLE TREE
BY THE WINDOW

I chopped down the big apple tree by the window.
It blocked the view, for one thing,
the living-room was dull in summer,
besides, the wholesalers no
longer wanted that kind of apple.
I thought of what my father
would have said, he liked
that apple tree.
But still I chopped it down.

It's much lighter, I
can see over the fjord
or keep an eye on
more neighbours,
the house is now in full
view, shows
more of itself.

I don't want to admit it, but I miss the apple tree.
Things are not the same. He gave good shelter
and good shade, the sun peeped through his branches
onto the table, and at night I often lay
listening to the airy leaves. And the apples –
none finer in spring, with their spicy taste.
It hurts each time I see the stump: when
it softens I'll hack it into firewood.

THE LOG-BOAT

A huge log came into view in a sand-bank
when they drained down the water.
There was something odd about it, and
when we dug it up it was a boat.
And a fine boat it had been, with
sheer in its lines – there
the thwart had been, there the rowlocks.
It had doubtless gone adrift sometime
or been left there by a fisherman,
just when, it was hard to say.
Now it lay there dark and glistening,
yes, it was fine, we wanted to come back
one day with a boat and fetch it.
We let it lie there on the sand in the sun.
When we came back, we said nothing, we didn't look
at the hollow cracked stump
as we drew it home over the water.

SUNNY DAY IN MARCH

Even the weathercock turns with the sun on such a
day.
It must be spring. Outside the cellar wall the cat
has found himself shelter. He's asleep, no doubt,
but his fur is well puffed up and his paws
well tucked under. A fly has been tempted out
from a crack in the warm plank wall – starts
buzzing. Soon stiffens. It's too cold.

THERE STANDS A HAZEL-STUMP

There stands a hazel-stump
among stones where the road
turns in to the yard.
A useless self-sown
hazel-stump.

One night I come home
two rowans are there.
They've stood there for ages,
crooked and wind-worn;
autumn it is,
their leaves rust-red.

Suddenly a tossing and
a singing and – two
green poplars soar
sky-high
on each side
of the gate.

In the dawn light I go out
and look, I liked
the old rowans.
No more than
the hazel-stump
to be seen.

A FARM HAS A BOW AND ARROW
AS ITS MARK

I have death in my point
behind greedy barbs,
sings the arrow.

I send the arrow
from the string,
quavers the bow.

Who draws the bow
if not I,
the strong arm?

Who found the bird,
aimed the arrow?
asks the eye.

I tense the arms,
I guide the eye,
says the will.

Take aim – fire!
It is my poison
that kills,
murmurs hunter's zeal.

That bird is mine,
I see it often,
reminds the dream.

And the bird vanished
on shy wings
in the sunless wood.

GEORG TRAKL

Childhood. A blue cave.
Wine. Verlaine.

Dreams and death. Poppies.
Madness.
Blood-stained snow.

Steel against bronze.
Hölderlin.

Not your dream. But
a betrayed black earth's:
cocaine.

WILLIAM BLAKE

What sort of trumpet is this
resounding so fully
in the morning sun,
what voice
so bold
and rousing?
Tiger, angel,
your fire
glows in secret,

wings folded
for feather-light gait.
I've long heard you
on earth
clear bright
among hoarse alp-horns and brassy bawling.

GÉRARD DE NERVAL

A burnt-out
body, can't he
dangle from a lamppost?

There remain
the light of the faithful eyes
and the voice of a heart
which has slept its diamond sleep.

THE LAST SPIDER

Above Sveig, so
   high
      the heather is about

to give up, I came upon
   the last
      spider, she

had hung herself
   in her own web.

Summer had been
   cold, not much
      in the way of midge
         or mosquito,

and the flies had
   stayed where
      things are fatter.

Yes, I came just to
   this rag of juniper, where
      a spider's web

hung and trembled
   in the autumn wind.

DEAD TREE

The magpie has flown,
she doesn't build in a dead tree.

LEAF-HUTS AND SNOW-HOUSES

There's not much to
these verses, only
a few words piled up
at random.
I think
nonetheless
it's fine
to make them, then
for a little while
I have something like a house.
I remember leaf-huts
we built
when we were small:
to creep in and sit
listening to the rain,
feel alone in the wilderness,
drops on your nose
and your hair –
Or snow-houses at Christmas,
to creep in and
close the hole with a sack,
light a candle and stay there
on cold evenings.

READ LU CHI AND MAKE A POEM

Read Lu Chi and make a poem.
He doesn't say what it should be like.
Many had painted an oak before.
Nonetheless Munch painted an oak.

I SEE YOU'VE LEARNT

I like
you
to use
few words,
few words and
short sentences
that drift
like a rain shower
down the page
with light and air
between.
I see you've learnt
to stack
a wood-pile in the forest,
good to build it
tall
then it'll dry;
if you build it long and low
the wood will rot.

A POEM EVERY DAY

I want to write a poem every day,
every day.
That should be easy enough.
Browning kept at it, though
he rhymed and
counted beats
with bushy eyebrows.
So, a poem a day.
Something strikes you,
something happens,
something catches your notice.
– I get up. It's light now.
I've the best intentions.
And see the bullfinch rising from the cherry tree,
where he's stealing my buds.

DON'T STAND THERE SHOUTING
ON A HILLTOP

Don't stand there
shouting on a hilltop.
Of course it's true,
what you say, so true
and such a racket
to make of it.
Get inside the hill,

make your smithy there,
build your forge there,
heat your iron there,
sing as you hammer!
We'll hear you,
hear you,
know where we have you.

I WAS SINGING OF A KINDLING-STICK

I was singing of
a kindling-stick,
now I sing of
a bumble-bee
that one day here
buzzed
in the bird-cherry
until un-
wittingly
it nudged against
the wooden wall
newly smeared
with tar.
Tough going,
said the bee.
Scratch your wings,
said the fly
on the butter.

THE OLD POET HAS MADE A VERSE

The old poet has made a verse.
And he's happy as a cider bottle
who in spring has sent
a fresh bubble up
and is about to pop the cork.

IN THE PARKER PEN

There are many verses in the Parker Pen, a whole
    kilometre,
and many more in the inkwell,
miles and miles. Papers
come in the post, bills, adverts, forms
to be filled up.
I face the future with confidence.

COLD DAY

The sun clenches his eye
behind a frozen crag.
The thermometer
creeps down and
down –
one's warmth
gathers
in a little
hollow.
I go easy on firewood,
keep the verse curt.

MIDWINTER. SNOW

Midwinter. Snow.
I give the birds a crust.
And sleep no worse for that.

AFTER WINTER

Tongue-tied forest beneath the stars.
In the quietness after winter.

Still no expectation,
no high excitement –
Will the spring-star take possession
or the darkness of winter?

In the forest floor streams are flowing.
The thrush has come.
Beneath the snow-crust
meagre grass stirs in the wind.

SNOWMEN IN A GREEN HAYFIELD

No one had expected the snow so early.
Children pulled out sledges, built snowmen and houses.
Today it's sunny and mild again. The snowmen
are still there, alone, weeping in a green hayfield.

BACK HOME

The magpies explode from the porch.
The cats scatter from corners.
The key is lying where I left it.

Dead flies on the sills.
The kettle cold and full of dregs.
In the drawer a hardened crust.
Tall goose-foot peeping in.

I HAVE LIVED HERE

I have lived here more than a generation.
Years with wind and stars in the high rigging
have sailed past.
Trees and birds have settled down here,
but I have not.

I LOOK AT THE POSTMARK ON YOUR FIRST LETTER

I look at the postmark on your first letter.
It's already a month since it arrived.
Since then you've haunted the house,
calling to me, startling me,
changing from Até to a green Erinys.
And today your photo came:
a pale girl sitting alone on some logs
at twilight by a darkening sea.

I AIM A LITTLE HIGH

For an arrow to hit the mark, it can't make
many detours. But a good archer
allows for the distance and the wind.
So when I aim at you, I aim a little high.

A LETTER'S COMING

A letter's coming.
And I'll be happy.
A wave of sorrow
carries me to the crest.

POOR OLD THING

Poor old thing
and infected with love!
See the glow in the cheeks,
and how the eyes glitter
with dead dreams!
An old birch soon gets
red marks meaning
'ready to fell'.

HORSES AND TRAMPS

Horses and tramps look for
roadside water-troughs.
What do they want
with petrol-stations?

THE LITTLE TIMBER SLEDGE

You're nothing but
    a little timber sledge
        hanging on to

the big timber sledge, you run
    in his tracks
        like a dog –

turn when he
    turns,
        stop

when he stops.
    But you are faithful,
        you carry what

they load on you,
    though you're spared
        the root-end

and the obligation
    to push your way through
        uncleared snow.

STRANGE FISH

Trust people?
One soon sees
what kind of strange
fish they are,
soon green,
soon black,
soon blue –
It's supposed to be
the light and the river-bed
and the current that
make them change colour.

HE'S A HUMAN BEING, LIKE YOU

You had respect for him
so long as you didn't
understand him or
grasp
what it was
he was at.
When you
did, that
was the end of your respect.

He's a human being,
like you,
and is trying to make of himself
a peacock.

THAT MAN

My old jacket
on a hook in the lean-to,
a pair of worn shoes,
I know
that man.

I flit him
to another peg,
another corner,
he's in the way.
I haven't had
the heart
to throw him
right out.

THERE ARE OMEN-BEARERS

There are omen-bearers:
wind, sprites, and birds.
And swing-doors.

Who
was it I saw
in the glass when
you came in?

The door swung to.
Neither of us
said a word.

WEIGHTS

Are you off on the space-trip
or are you
one of those weights
that stay on the ground and say
that'll never get up.

There's nothing to be done with weights.
They stand there.
You can weigh them, they'll
not mind.

But they'll stand there
just as unyielding, just as cold.

They're the ones who know
how heavy things are.

THE CHRISTMAS SHEAF

No great
shakes this
year, your
Christmas sheaf,
grain gone
green and mouldy in your barn.

But up goes
your sheaf
on a stake
– high – and you
expect thanks
both from the birds and from Our Lord.

YOU DON'T HANG YOUR HAT ON A SUNBEAM

You must without fail have
firm ground
under your feet, something

to hold on to,
thought
doesn't dare

let go,
is like a child,
doesn't trust itself but

without fail fumbles for
something to hold.
You don't hang

your hat
on a sunbeam,
you were late

learning to swim,
you distrust flying,
don't feel safe

except on foot.

I LOSE MYSELF IN DAYDREAMS

I lose myself in day-dreams
here in the farthest hayfield,
in groves of hogweed
and fern.
Round the tufts of hair-grass
swirl butterflies
more beautiful than
birds of paradise,
and I'm a child again
and away and
one
with fragrant grass
and sailing clouds –
Until
a raw wind
shakes
a solitary
pine-sized
bracken-top
and ants
creep
under my clothes.

NO CAR, NO PLANE

No car,
no plane –
either a hay-sledge
or a rattletrap
– or Elijah's fiery chariot.

You'll not get further than Bashō.
He got there on foot.

AN ORDER HAS GONE OUT

An order has gone out
that all the world's diamonds
be counted in the census
and be set to cutting glass.

I'M DRIFTING

I'm drifting, driven
by wind, by waves.
I've clambered up on a log,
and I'm proud that it's carved.

THE ROAD ROLLER

It gives you due warning at the bend,
comes towards you in the half-light,
fiery horns
blinking from its forehead –
comes heavily, comes rolling authoritatively,
smoothing out the asphalt strip you must follow.

Everyone must stay on the asphalt strips,
the conveyor-belts running from
maternity ward to crematorium.

I LOOK AT AN OLD MIRROR

On the front a mirror.
On the back a picture of the Garden of Eden.

A fanciful conceit
of the old glass-master.

FROM WAR-TIME

A bullet stotted onto my floor.
I weighed it in my hand.
It had come through the window
and two wooden walls.
I didn't doubt it could kill.

THE DECEMBER MOON 1969

He hides the steel
in a silver scabbard.
There's blood on the edge.

NEW YEAR 1970

A minister's wife in black has come
unannounced to the farm.
And a yellow wolf.

I LOOK OVER THE SCYTHES BEFORE MOWING

Used scythes
always shine,
never rust, although
I see these too are done.
Which is best, rusting unused in the box
or worn out by whetstone and rocky hay-patch?

SOLITARY PINE

Plenty of space here, you've been able to
stretch up and spread your crown
wide.

But you stand alone.
When the storms come, you have
no one to lean on.

ASK THE WIND

Ask the wind,
the lighter the better.
He travels far
and often comes back
with a good answer.

MOUNTAINS NO LONGER ENTICE ME

Mountains no longer entice me.
I've lived long enough among cold glaciers.
I still make my way through the woods, listen
to the autumn wind, pause by the tarns,
follow the rivers. Even late in the year
you can find berries there.
If you want to get further you'll have to cross
     mountains.
Let the peaks stand where they are as bearings.

MANY YEARS' EXPERIENCE
WITH BOW AND ARROW

It's the black dot right
in the middle you're to hit,
right there, where
the arrow will stand trembling!
But just there is where you don't hit.
You're close, closer, no,
not close enough.
So it's off to pick the arrows up,
walk back, try again.
The black dot teases you.
Until you understand the arrow
that stands there trembling:
here too is a mid-point.

I EMPTY THE ASH-DRAWER

A few wakeful stars are hanging above the mountains
when I step out. Between pine trunks the pale
snow-crust is glimmering in the spring light.
The embers sizzle in the snow when I empty the ash-
    drawer.
Crumbling dreams scatter with the ashes in grey wind.

NEW TABLE-CLOTH

New yellow cloth on the table.
And clean white pages!
Here the words must come,
such a fine new cloth here
and such fine paper!
The ice settled on the fjord,
the birds came and alighted.

TWO BOATS ON THE FJORD

Two boats side by side out on the fjord.
A fisherman on each and lines out.
The same fjord, the same fine weather for both.
When one pulls a fish in over the side
the other can well wonder why
didn't it take my hook?
Such thoughts they have on such a fine day.

I'LL HAVE TO THINK OF DOING
SOMETHING WRONG

Too happy by half –
the kettle's on the boil,
one scale-arm's sky-high!
I'll have to think of doing something wrong,
throw cold water on the kettle,
hang a stone on the scales,
fell the biggest pine I've got.

UP THROUGH THE RIVER VALLEY

I step lightly on the stones,
fresh rivery gust against me,
and I sing.
Sorrow is the well of strength,
the glaciers weep in the sun,
why do I walk more lightly
against than with?

EVENING SERVICE

The Evangelists hang in the chancel
and hear their own words from the pulpit.
The candles flicker on the altar
in shadowy rings of doubt.
The congregation try to sing true
right up under the high roof.

COMPANY

You like best
talking with the wind,
having him
for company.

Or trees, homely,
assured,
wise trees.

But having me
for company?
It's good
you're used
to ghosts.

TO A LADY WHO SENT ME A RECORD
OF BACH AND HANDEL

What would Wang Wei have done if you'd sent
him a record of Bach and Handel?
He'd have played the sonatas over and over
in his hut by Wang River in Chungnan
and dreamt himself away to his white clouds.
Then he'd have made a poem and sent it to you.
It would have pleased not only you but posterity as
well.
My poem, it'll be only you, Bodil, who'll read it.

SLEEP

Let's glide into
sleep, into
the calm dream,
glide in – two
lumps of dough in
the good oven
called night.
And then waken
in the morning
two round
golden loaves!

THE RIVER MURMURS

Leaves come,
    twigs and rubbish,
        brushwood and stumps –

I carry it all gladly
    on my back
        as long as I can,

when I can't, any more,
    I dump it, it
        can just wait there

for some other time.
    I'm most grateful
        for ground-water and brooks,

they add to my strength.
    If a wild tributary comes
        dancing

the very breath is
    knocked out of me,
        we arch our backs

and bicker and bicker, which
    holds course,
        which gives way?

I PAUSE BENEATH A LAMPPOST
ONE SNOWY EVENING

At last, there I see
    the solitary lamppost
        where the road divides,

steadfastly holding up
    its umbrella of light
        in the snowy evening.

I pause, although I don't have
    any love-letter
        I shyly

should have read, it just
    seems curious
        pausing here

under the umbrella when
    the snow's so thick,
        and watching how

the flakes hover
    for a little
        in the ring of light

before they whirl back
    to the darkness or
        glide quietly down.

And round me in the darkness
    — snow, snow.

EGIL

If you didn't have a hauberk to hand
you'd rope a flagstone to your chest,
if you didn't have a sword
you'd grab a cudgel.
I believe you had your eyes about you
where you walked.
But when you made poems
you'd spread your sheepskin
over your head.

PAUL CELAN

Shut inside this rotating
ghost-house, life,
with little openings each
giving on
its own reality
– we live,
are at home here –
most of us gather
at the biggest one,
this is the world,
we say.

At yours
sat
only you –
eye black
diamond,
heart
a bloodstone.

AFTER READING GUILLEVIC

After reading
Guillevic
you are not
full
but a
green, greedy
lupin
in river sand.

THE BIG SCALES

It's the old scales
that matter most
in the warehouse here
(along with me of course),
which is why their place is
the middle of the floor, it's
up to them to tell
how heavy things are, to settle
how much they'll cost to send.
True – I can feel
when I heave crates and sacks
how heavy they are,
but they must onto the scales
to let them have their word.
We negotiate, the scales and I,

while I add the weights,
and more often than not
we agree – they tip,
I nod,
and we say
'That's it' – no need
to count every gram.
The scales are rusty and my
back arthritic;
happily the weights are
lighter than the things I weigh.
At times I notice people doubt
my accuracy.
People are odd.
If they're selling something
it must be heavy,
if they're sending something
it must be light.
The magistrate was in one day,
he too gazed at the scales, no doubt
remembering what
he has to weigh.
'They're not dispensing scales,' I said,
though what I had in mind was a pair
I saw in the goldsmith's,
he was weighing gold-dust
with tweezers.
Besides, I've often thought of what
a magistrate has to weigh:
right and wrong,
punishments and fines,
lives and fates.
Who adjusts
those weights,
those scales?

MOUNTAINS ARE HEAVY THINGS TO MOVE

Mountains are heavy things to move,
oak-root won't budge,
who dares take issue
with the big things of the world?
Oxes and elephants bear them on their backs
on long journeys, eagles toss out
bloody chunks and swoop
to rock walls and ravines,
the wolves dog-fight over them,
the foxes slink round the bait,
the flies leave them filthy,
the magpie steals the silver,
the serpent wears the crown.

BAROMETER

The gilded arrow
I can
flit at will
– I'd like it
to stay at
good weather.

The black arrow
I have no
power over – it
obeys without mercy
cosmic forces;
grudgingly
I turn
the gilded arrow
after it.

I'd rather leave it
at
good weather
– hoping that
the black arrow
will have to come
back.

HOW LONG HAVE YOU BEEN SLEEPING?

You actually dare
to open your eyes
and look about you?
Oh yes, you're here,
here in this world,
you're not dreaming,
it's like this, the way
you're seeing it, things here
are like this.
This?
Oh yes, just like this,
no other way.
How long have you been sleeping?

IT'S HIGH TIME

Rockets stick
their snouts up
and aim at the moon and Mars.
It's time
high time
to sow their poison among the stars.

BEFORE THE LAST DAY

Christ's words
and the gruel of Heraclitus
can still save the world.
– Simple as that.

STARE MIASTO

(the old part of Warsaw)

You feel shameful here.
What feckless folk
do you come from?
A people free for a century
and they haven't yet rebuilt
one cathedral, still less their language.

A proud people remember their tyrants.
And Sigismund Vasa
is back on his column in Zamkowy Square.

It's not to honour kings and prelates
they've built the city again stone by stone,
but for the unknown hands that slaved
under them, and still found joy in the making.

SNOW IN CASTILLE

In Castille they welcome the snow – with the same
    delight
as we greet the blossoming fruit trees in spring.
That's why Machado sings so sweetly of snow,
snow on the sunburnt rusty hills of Castille!
A shadow sleeps under the snow on the olive branches
– I remember the gardens at home, often bitten
    by frost.

I PASS THE ARCTIC CIRCLE

A man on the train points at the mountain cairn,
we're passing the arctic circle, he says.
At first we can't see any difference,
landscape the same, to the north,
but we do know what we're going towards.
I wouldn't have noticed this small event
if I hadn't, one of these days, passed seventy.

I PAUSE BENEATH THE OLD OAK
ONE RAINY DAY

It's not just the rain
that makes me pause
beneath the old oak
by the roadside, it feels
safe beneath the broad
crown, it must be
old friendship that lets
the oak and me stand there
silent, listening to the rain
drip in the leaves, looking out
in the grey day,
waiting, understanding.
The world is old, we think,
and we're both ageing.
Today I'm not standing dry,
the leaves have taken to falling,
there's a sour smell in
the raw air, I feel
through my hair.

LEAVES LOOSEN

Let him have them,
　　thinks the birch, and
　　　　gives the wind free play

with the yellow leaves –
　　left standing naked
　　　　and cold in thin twigs.

Nothing like it,
　　being poor,
　　　　no better

place to stand on
　　than bare rock
　　　　either.

The oak naked now too
　　but not poor.
　　　　Wisely sucked out

strength from leaves before
　　letting them one
　　　　by one go,

has long since been asleep
　　under grey bark,
　　　　knuckled branches

poking in the night
　　for stars,
　　　　and the roots pierce deep

in sheltering mould.

A world of modern poets from Anvil

Guillaume Apollinaire
Ana Blandiana
Johannes Bobrowski
Elisabeth Borchers
Bei Dao
Josep Carner
Nina Cassian
Paul Celan
Jibanananda Das
Ştefan Aug. Doinaş
Odysseus Elytis
Nikos Gatsos
Nikolay Gumilyov
Nâzım Hikmet
Peter Huchel
Sarah Kirsch
Ivan V Lalić
Federico García Lorca
Pablo Neruda
Justo Jorge Padrón
János Pilinszky
Vasko Popa
Rainer Maria Rilke
Yannis Ritsos
Tadeusz Różewicz
George Seferis
Vittorio Sereni
Rabindranath Tagore

www.anvilpresspoetry.com